YES

Life is waiting. Are you ready?

WRITTEN BY: Robi Yamada

DESIGNED BY: Jessica Phoenix

There will always be CRITICS.

AND WHILE THEY CAN COME IN MANY FORMS, THE ONES "OUT THERE" ARE SOMETIMES NOTHING COMPARED TO THE CRITICS IN OUR OWN HEADS. AS WE ALL KNOW, WE CAN BE HARD ON OURSELVES.

DOUBTS, FEARS, AND NEGATIVITY ARE PART OF LIFE AND CAN AT TIMES FEEL INSURMOUNTABLE. SOMETIMES ALL WE HEAR IS THE NEGATIVE; WE FOCUS ON THE CRITICAL THINGS "THEY" SAY ABOUT US. BUT WHO ARE "THEY" ANYWAY? WHY DO WE GIVE THEM ANY POWER?

WHY WOULD WE BELIEVE THE WORST
THAT IS SAID ABOUT US INSTEAD OF
TRUSTING THE BEST THAT IS INSIDE
OF US?

The key is to **BELIEVE** *in* *yourself,*
TO TRUST THE POTENTIAL THAT IS
INSIDE OF YOU, AND TO PUT IT INTO
EVERYTHING THAT YOU DO. BECAUSE
THIS IS IT. YOU ONLY LIVE ONCE.
AND WHILE YOU MAY NOT BE ABLE
TO DETERMINE THE LENGTH OF YOUR
LIFE, YOU CAN DO PLENTY ABOUT
HOW YOU CHOOSE TO LIVE IT.

LIFE IS WAITING... RIGHT HERE, RIGHT
NOW. ARE YOU READY? *(Say YES.)*

THEY WILL TELL YOU

NO.

They will tell you that

they have concerns.

They will say that

you're not

quite right

or

not good enough.

They will explain that

they just don't

want you to be

disappointed.

THEY WILL SAY
YOU'RE NOT THAT
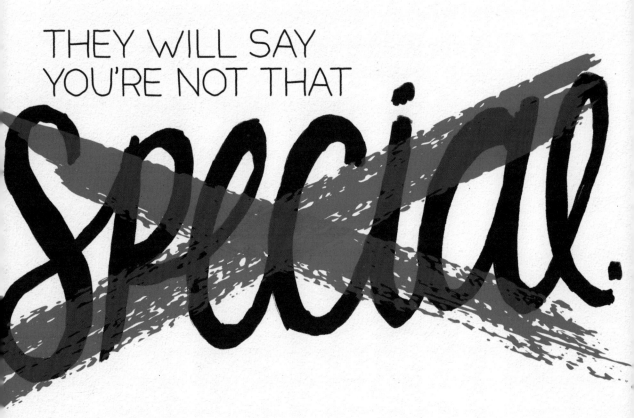

WILL YOU TELL THEM THAT
WHAT THIS WORLD NEEDS

are people who

DOUBT

their

DOUBTS

MORE THAN THEY

FEAR

their

FEARS?

THEY WILL TELL YOU
THAT YOU
DON'T
HAVE WHAT IT
TAKES.

THEY WILL TELL YOU TO GIVE UP. THEY WILL TELL YOU IT'S JUST NOT POSSIBLE.

Will you tell them that THE WORLD IS FILLED with countless examples of those who have BEATEN unbelievably LONG ODDS?

THEY WILL
TELL YOU THAT
YOU JUST
DON'T
MEASURE UP.

WILL YOU TELL THEM THAT REALITY IS IN THE EYE OF THE BEHOLDER, *and that* NO TWO PEOPLE EVER SEE ANYTHING IN EXACTLY THE SAME WAY?

Will you tell them that by seeing the **GOOD** in others, you are also helping to create it?

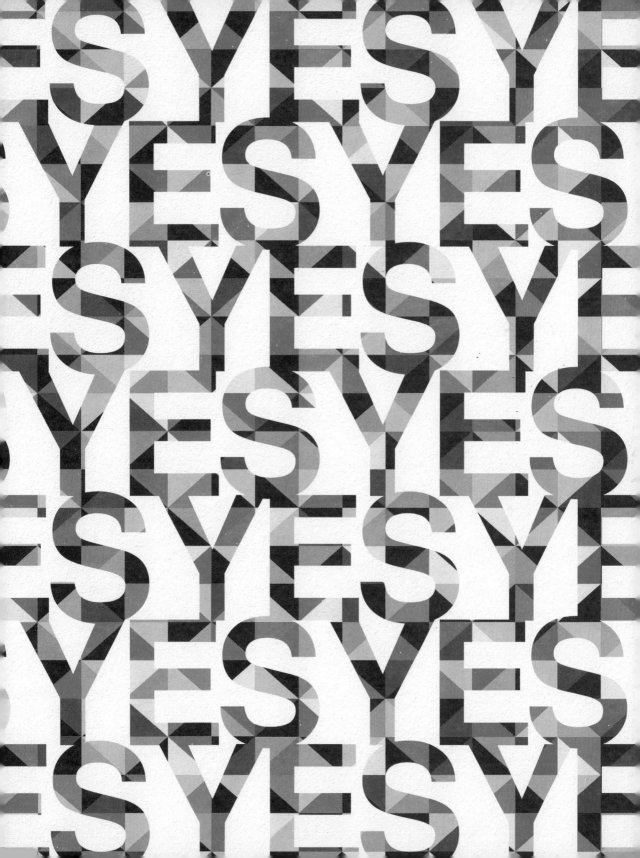

They will tell you that you

☑ **AREN'T QUALIFIED ENOUGH**

or that

☑ **YOU ARE TOO SMART FOR YOUR OWN GOOD.**

They will tell you that

IT JUST
ISN'T
MEANT
TO BE.

They will explain that it's **BAD LUCK** or poor timing.

They will tell you that

LIFE'S
not
FAIR.

Will you tell
them that
the future is
built by faith,
optimism, &
perseverance?

Will you tell them that life isn't only how you take it, but also what you make it?

They will tell you to

NOT GET YOUR *HOPES* UP.

Will you tell them that THE MOST PRACTICAL thing in the WORLD is to DO what you LOVE?

WILL YOU TELL THEM THAT
YOU WOULD RATHER
*aim too high
& miss,*

THAN
*aim too low
& hit?*

THEY WILL TELL
YOU TO GET
SERIOUS.
THEY WILL TELL YOU TO
BE PRACTICAL &
QUIT DREAMING.

THEY WILL TELL YOU

Will you tell them that
LIFE IS
FUN &
you don't want
TO MISS
ANYTHING?

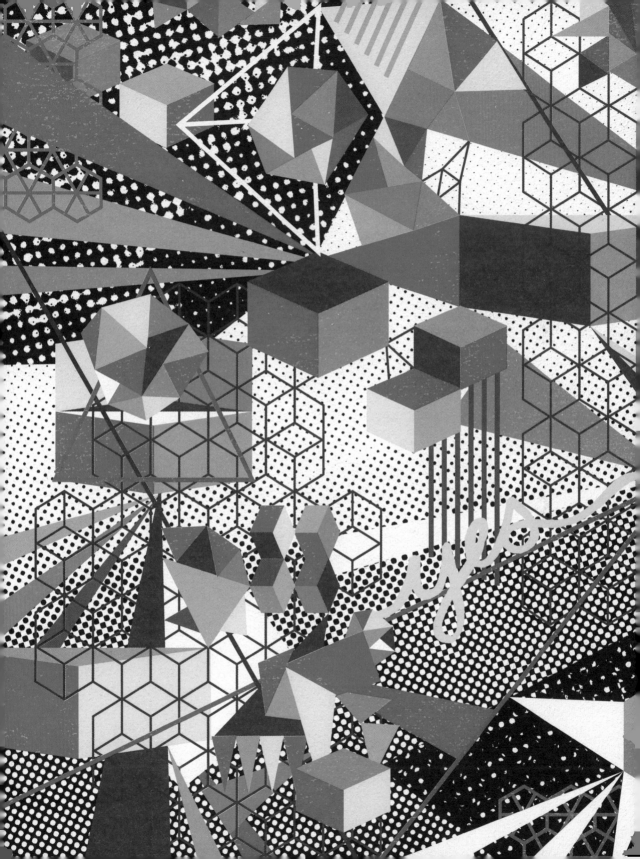

WILL YOU TELL THEM THAT EVERY DAY
IS HERE TO BE ENJOYED BECAUSE

VERY MOMENT, EVERY OPPORTUNITY,
T WILL NEVER COME AGAIN?

will you tell them that no one in the entire history of the universe has ever been or will ever be, exactly & uniquely, like you?

THEY
WILL ASK
WHAT MAKES
YOU SO SURE.
THEY WILL
SAY IT'S
TOO RISKY
AND THAT
YOU SHOULD
PLAY IT
SAFE.

THEY WIL
TELL YOU
TO QUIT
WHILE
YOU'RE
AHEAD

WILL YOU TELL THEM THAT TAKING

RISKS MAKES YOU FEEL *alive*?

They will tell you that

NOW

is just not the time.

Will you tell them that

TODAY IS

THE DAY

and that there will never be a day when it's not today?

THEY WILL TELL YOU

NO.

Author's Note:

THIS BOOK WAS INSPIRED BY A NIKE PRINT
AD I SAW BACK IN THE MID-1990s ABOUT
SELF-BELIEF AND NOT TAKING NO FOR
AN ANSWER. IT STUCK WITH ME AND HAS
BEEN AN INSPIRATION FOR ME EVER SINCE.
IT IS IN HOMAGE TO THAT SPIRIT AND
CREATIVITY THAT THIS BOOK WAS WRITTEN.

*In honor of Bob Moawad, who always
lived life "positively."*

COMPENDIUM®
live inspired.

With special thanks to the entire Compendium family.

CREDITS:
WRITTEN BY: KOBI YAMADA
DESIGNED BY: JESSICA PHOENIX
EDITED BY: M.H. CLARK & AMELIA RIEDLER
CREATIVE DIRECTION BY: JULIE FLAHIFF

LIBRARY OF CONGRESS CONTROL NUMBER: 2014943679
ISBN: 978-1-938298-53-0